BECOME A LISTENING EAR

BY

OMAR LILES

DEDICATION

I want to dedicate this book foremost to my mother, Linda Williams, and to my brothers and sisters from the Liles, Green, Thomas, and Irvin families. I also would like to thank my mentors, who have been a significant part of my life and have gone to heaven. Rev. Dr. Leora Liggins from Christ Resurrection Missionary Baptist Church has played a great role in my life and has trained me in ministry. I also would like to thank Dr. Malachi Brantley for helping me grow in ministry and for allowing me to preach at Shiloh Baptist Church in Newark, NJ. I would like to thank my friends, whom I consider like brothers and sisters: Minister Latisha Bearfield, Keisha Natalee Cole, Stanley Adams, Suzette DeCruize, and Dr. Keith and Tiffany Wilkes from CTC Church, for allowing me to take part in many aspects of ministry and for establishing the Kingdom School of Divinity.

FORWARD

In a world that incessantly buzzes with noise, distractions, and relentless demands for attention, the art of truly listening—of being a genuine, empathetic ear for those in need—has become a rare gift. "Becoming A Listening Ear" by Omar Liles emerges as a beacon of hope for anyone yearning to master this lost art, and for those seeking solace in being understood, not just heard. This book is not merely a guide; it is a journey into the heart of what it means to listen, to empathize, and to offer the kind of support that can truly transform lives.

The essence of Liles' writing resonates with a universal truth: at the core of our being, each of us longs to be seen, to be acknowledged, and to be validated. In the hustle of our daily lives, where everyone seems to be speaking but few genuinely listen, the yearning for a listening ear becomes more acute, more poignant. Liles taps into this deep-seated need, exploring the profound impact that attentive listening can have on individuals, couples, and young adults alike. The narrative woven throughout this book sheds light on the simple, yet profound, notion that to be listened to is to be cared for deeply, beyond the surface level of casual conversation.

"Becoming A Listening Ear" delves into the myriad reasons why people feel unheard and the societal tendencies that contribute to this disconnect. It addresses the hesitancy many feel towards seeking professional help, driven by fears of being judged, diagnosed, or overwhelmed with questions. Liles offers insights into the nuanced dynamics of listening—not as a passive act, but as an active, intentional gesture of compassion and understanding. Through personal anecdotes, theoretical perspectives, and practical advice, the book encourages readers to cultivate their ability to listen, to understand, and to connect with others on a level that transcends words.

Moreover, Liles confronts the challenges and pitfalls that come with trying to find a genuine listener in a world where attention is fragmented. The book acknowledges the pain of sharing one's most vulnerable secrets, only to have them dismissed or, worse, used against them. It is a call to rediscovery, urging readers to rekindle the empathy and attentiveness that form the bedrock of meaningful human connection.

"Becoming A Listening Ear" is more than a book; it is a manifesto for change—a call to action for anyone who believes in the transformative power of being present for someone else. It champions the idea that, in a world eager to speak, the greatest gift we can offer is our silence, our attention, and our willingness to understand the stories of those around us. As you turn the pages, you may find yourself on a path not just to becoming a better listener, but to becoming a beacon of hope and understanding in the lives of those you encounter.

Welcome to a journey that promises to enrich your relationships, deepen your empathy, and remind you of the power of listening. Welcome to "Becoming A Listening Ear."

The Celebs Life Coach,
Takiyah Diamond

ABOUT THE AUTHOR

Omar Liles is a certified Dementia Practitioner with The National Council of Certified Dementia Practitioners and a graduate of New York Divinity School with a Master of Religion at City Vision University.

He studied at Eastern Theological Seminary and attended Andersonville Theological Seminary with a Doctor of Ministry and currently training as a professional chaplain and Pastoral Care Counseling in Psychotherapy with the College of Pastoral Supervision and Psychotherapy. A graduate of New Skills Academy with certification in Life and Mental Health Coaching. He attended Light University with training in Mental Health Coaching with specialization in trauma and life coaching. He trained in Dementia with the Center of Applied Research in Dementia.

He appeared on various platforms such as podcasts, radio shows, and panel's that focused on Grief, Mental Health Awareness, Singleness, Alzheimer's and Dementia, Ministry, Biblical Counseling and Coaching. Cofounder of Kingdom School of Divinity

TABLE OF CONTENTS

INTRODUCTION

The writing within this book will be based on issues that's so important to everyday people who just want someone to share what they have to say to someone that they feel comfortable with. The primary focus would be on having a listening ear. We all would love to have someone to go to in our lives when we feel like no one else is listening to us. In different circumstances if we do go to someone who happens to be a professional many are hesitant to attend a session because of the fear that they will be bombarded with a thousand questions, being diagnosed, or labeled when all we want to be is heard from the presence of someone who will take the time to listen to what we have to say. Sometimes we make the mistake and share our life experiences with people who don't want to listen and if they do listen it will go out of one ear and out the other. It is as if they never heard us at all. When all we're doing is sharing our feelings and emotions about a particular circumstance within our lives, we are looking for that person who has a listening ear for conversation and to help us with our goals to get us from one place to another in our lives. Some individuals, couples and young adults will even seek out professional help and they may not be that much help as well as seemed that having a listening ear has been a lost art among many.

One of the reasons why is because too many people are listening to more than one person at the same time or the person who is the listener is not showing care. We have listened to so many people that have not shown any sort of love concerning the stories and the issues that we have that we are willing to sacrifice to tell them even if we believe that they weren't going to tell anyone. And too often many have fallen into the hands of prey to those that they have told their dearest and most vulnerable secrets too. Let's discuss having a listening ear.

TRUSTWORTHY LISTENER

God, no matter how omniscient He is, listens to every word we speak. He understands the therapeutic effect of having Him listen to us when we speak. He also allows us to know intricate details of other people's lives at times, so we can pay attention. We've seen both the good and the bad effects of listening, depending on what we do with what we are told. Being a bad steward of the thing others tell us causes more damage than what is there already. Listening is an art that not only involves inclining an ear to the words of the sharer, but also directing our attitude towards a problem-solving approach.

Perhaps you should be a bit more attentive to the unvocalized message that someone is communicating when they choose to trust you with details about their lives. They are not only asking for help, but also communicating just how highly they esteem you. Whatever you do with the information shared elevates or nullifies the high esteem in which you are regarded.

Being trustworthy is one of the most elemental virtues of listening. It communicates a presence of empathy and goodwill towards the person sharing. Haven't you noticed that a person could be suffering alone in silence despite being surrounded by many people? It isn't about numbers or availability, but virtue. Wouldn't you rather wait for a trusted friend that is miles away than confide in your neighbor when you have a pressing issue? Do you have trustworthy listeners in your life? Are you a trustworthy listener?

To be an effective problem solver, you must be a thorough listener to make judgments based on full information and without partiality. Good listeners are easily interpreted to be wise even when they have nothing to say. Why so? Because it is typical of wisdom to talk less and listen more.

Lack Of Understanding

The word lack of understanding? It means "incomprehension. noun. the condition of not being able to understand." *macmilliandictionary.com*

Many of us go through many days of our lives not having anyone to understand why we behave the way we do because of their lack of understanding. Many people who go through not being understood are often looked at as the problem of being damaged. Lack of understanding drives them through the roof, in other words their patience has often come to an end with the person in whom they have confided with so they look for someone who can. We need to get to a point where we can safely talk about our problems with more unashamed conversation with people who love us. When you lack mutual understanding in a relationship you lose the essence of why you are together, and your happiness begins to dim. So many couples go through problems where they cannot understand one another. If couples fail to understand one another our relationships fail. This is why counseling is important. It's important for people in general who are looking for change in their lives. Change within families and communities. It helps navigate through the difficulties in life situations, from the loss of loved ones, broken relationships or the experience of trauma.

Lack of understanding can lead to conflict, and relational growth with spouses, friends and family. Getting some form of coaching or counseling will help us understand who we are and how to make true connections with people we know.

When We Lack Communication in Relationships

Escalated conflict can happen. Develop a negative perspective of your spouse, friend or family member. Feeling unseen or unknown Loneliness.

THE SILENT STRUGGLE:
UNRAVELING THE PROFOUND EFFECTS OF NOT BEING HEARD

Have you felt like your voice didn't matter? Like no one is listening to you. If so, you're not alone. Not being heard is a common experience that can affect everyone's lives.

In a world where opinions and ideas are meant to be shared and sometimes challenged, the feeling of not being heard can be disheartening. This subject delves into the effects of not being heard. We aim to inspire a collective call for a more inclusive and empathetic society.

THE PSYCHOLOGICAL IMPACT OF NOT BEING HEARD

The feeling of not being listened to can leave deep emotional scars silently festering within individuals. When we're not heard, it can be emotionally devastating. We may feel frustrated, angry, and helpless. Oftentimes, we start doubting ourselves and our worth.

A study by the University of California, Berkeley found that people who felt unheard were more likely to experience symptoms of depression, anxiety, and post-traumatic stress disorder (PTSD). They were also more likely to have low self-esteem and to feel isolated and alone.

The study also found that people who felt unheard were more likely to engage in self-destructive behaviors, such as substance abuse, self-harm, and have suicidal thoughts and attempts.

When perspectives, concerns, and ideas are consistently dismissed or ignored, it chips away at our self-esteem. The absence of validation and acknowledgment creates a sense of invisibility and feeds into feelings of unworthiness. Over time, this can lead to a loss of identity and a disconnection from our thoughts and emotions.

Moreover, the psychological impact extends beyond the individual. When a person's voice is silenced repeatedly, they may internalize a belief that their opinions are insignificant, stifling their ability to express themselves fully in any context. This suppression can contribute to a cycle of self-censorship, where individuals refrain from speaking up even when it matters most.

THE SOCIAL IMPACT OF NOT BEING HEARD

Beyond the individual level, the repercussions of not being heard can be felt even through interpersonal relationships and wider societal dynamics. Without a receptive audience, communication and connection falter, fostering feelings of isolation and loneliness.

When individuals are not heard, a breakdown in relationships occurs. The lack of open and honest dialogue inhibits the formation of deep connections as trust erodes and misunderstandings prevail. Without the opportunity to be heard and understood, relationships may be impacted, leading to distance and isolation.

A study by the University of Michigan found that people who felt unheard were more likely to have conflicts with their partners, friends, and family members.

They were also more likely to feel like they didn't belong and didn't have a voice in their relationships. The study also found that people who felt unheard were more likely to be victims of abuse and neglect. They were also more likely to have difficulty forming and maintaining healthy relationships.

On a larger scale, the suppression of diverse voices hampers progress and impedes the collective ability to address critical social issues and make informed decisions. A society that values and encourages active listening and diverse perspectives fosters innovation, inclusivity, and social cohesion. Conversely, when marginalized voices are silenced or ignored, the full spectrum of human experiences remains untapped, limiting our understanding and hindering societal growth.

THE PROFESSIONAL IMPACT OF NOT BEING HEARD

The workplace, too, becomes a battleground for those who remain unheard. The lack of recognition and validation can affect our overall job satisfaction and motivation, resulting in decreased productivity and diminished innovation.

Employees may feel demoralized and disengaged in a work environment where individuals' voices are not valued. Employees become disenchanted when ideas and contributions go unnoticed or unappreciated, decreasing job satisfaction. The lack of fulfillment stifles creativity and productivity, hindering the organization's success.

A study by the University of Pennsylvania found that people who felt unheard at work were more likely to experience burnout, turnover, and job dissatisfaction. The study revealed that they were more likely to have lower levels of job performance and has also found that people who felt unheard at work were likelier to be passed over for promotions and opportunities. They were also more likely to be laid off or terminated.

These feelings can also impact levels of creativity and professional growth, which leads to individuals to miss out on career advancement and skill development opportunities. When promotions, raises, and options for growth are allocated based on favoritism rather than merit or the quality of ideas, talented individuals are relegated to the sidelines. Feelings of being underappreciated can potentially affect individuals and deprive organizations of diverse perspectives and innovate solutions.

STRATEGIES FOR OVERCOMING THE EFFECTS OF NOT BEING HEARD

While the effects of not being heard can be discouraging, there are proactive steps we and the communities can take to overcome this silent struggle.

Building Effective Communication Skills

Effective communication skills involve learning to express oneself clearly and assertively while actively listening to others. By understanding communication, individuals can navigate conversations more effectively and increase their chances of being heard.

Cultivating Self-Confidence

Cultivating self-confidence is crucial for overcoming the psychological impacts of not being heard. Recognizing one's worth, acknowledging strengths, and celebrating achievements are key steps toward developing a strong sense of self. When individuals believe in themselves and their ideas, they are more likely to speak up and be heard.

Advocating for Oneself

Advocating for oneself means actively asserting one's needs, concerns, and opinions. This involves setting boundaries, standing up for oneself when necessary, and seeking support from allies or mentors who can amplify one's voice. Through self-advocacy, individuals can break the cycle of silence and claim their rightful place in conversations and decision-making processes.

Simultaneously, creating inclusive environments that encourage active listening and empathy is crucial for ensuring the diverse voices within a community are genuinely heard and respected. Cultivating a culture of respect, inclusivity, and openness to different perspectives fosters an environment where everyone feels safe to speak up and contribute. Active listening, empathy, and valuing diverse opinions are essential skills that can be cultivated within communities, organizations, and society at large.

In addition, to these strategies, here are some other things you can do to overcome the effects of not being heard:

Seek professional help: If you're struggling to cope with the emotional impact of not being heard, you may want to seek professional help from a therapist or counselor.

Join a support group: Many support groups are available for people who have experienced the effects of not being heard. Joining a support group can provide you with a safe space to share your experiences and connect with others who understand what you're going through.

Take care of yourself: When feeling unheard, taking care of yourself physically and emotionally is important. This means eating healthy, getting enough sleep, and exercising regularly. It also means finding activities that you enjoy and that help you relax and de-stress.

Be patient: Overcoming the effects of not being heard takes time. Don't get discouraged if you don't see results immediately. Just keep practicing the strategies you've learned; eventually, you'll feel heard and valued.

Aside from helping individuals overcome the effects of not being heard, it's also important to create inclusive environments where everyone's voices are valued. This means encouraging active listening and empathy and fostering a culture that values diversity of thought. Here are some tips for creating inclusive environments:

Encourage active listening: Active listening means paying attention to the speaker, understanding their point of view, and asking clarifying questions. It also means avoiding interrupting the speaker and judging their ideas.

Foster empathy: Empathy means understanding and sharing the feelings of another person. It means putting yourself in their shoes and trying to see things from their perspective.

Value diversity of thought: Diversity of thought means valuing different perspectives and ideas. It means creating a space where everyone feels comfortable sharing their opinions, even if they differ from the majority.

The profound effects of not being heard are a call to action for society. We must recognize the emotional toll it takes on individuals and its limitations on collective progress. By fostering a culture that values and embraces diverse voices, we can create a world where everyone's contributions are acknowledged. Let's be more empathic and understanding because being heard should not be a luxury but a fundamental right.

In our quest for a more inclusive and compassionate society, let us dismantle the barriers that silence voices, empowering each other to speak up, be heard, and collectively shape a brighter future. By embracing the power of listening and providing platforms for all voices to be heard, we can forge stronger connections, cultivate innovation, and pave the way for a more equitable world where everyone's voice matters.

If you're feeling unheard, there are things you can do to change that. You can start by developing effective communication skills, building self-confidence, and creating inclusive environments. You can also reach out to others who have experienced the same thing and find support.

REFERENCES:

Brosh, C. by A. (2015, August 10). *GoodTherapy.org*. Good Therapy. https://www.goodtherapy.org/blog/listen-up-why-you-dont-feel-heard-in-your-relationship-0810154

Elizabeth Scott, P. (n.d.). *The very real effects of relationship conflict and stress*. Very well Mind. https://www.verywellmind.com/the-toll-of-conflict-in-relationships-3144952

Klare Heston, L. (2019, March 29). *3 ways to cope with not feeling heard*. wikiHow. https://www.wikihow.com/Cope-with-Not-Feeling-Heard

The power of talk: Who gets heard and why. Harvard Business Review. (2019, October 15). https://hbr.org/1995/09/the-power-of-talk-who-gets-heard-and-why

Raypole, C. (2021, May 28). *How to be seen and heard when you're feeling invisible*. Psych Central. https://psychcentral.com/depression/how-to-be-seen-and-heard-when-youre-feeling-invisible

Why it's so hard to speak up against a toxic culture. Harvard Business Review. (2020, October 30). https://hbr.org/2018/05/why-its-so-hard-to-speak-up-against-a-toxic-culture

Why we need to feel heard. The School of Life. (n.d.). https://www.theschooloflife.com/article/why-we-need-to-feel-heard/

Listening To Make Sound Decisions

When a person makes sound decisions, they can assess any given situation with judgment based on their experiences. Decision making is part of a person's everyday life whether it's on the job dealing with their finances or in their relationships. When an individual chooses not to listen to their spouse, coach, friend or counselor they are making the choice to do wrong in their life and because of this they will make unsound decisions that will cause trouble and leave them into a chaotic situation without using the wisdom that was given to them. They have not taken careful consideration to pray, read scripture or ask God for direction. Sometimes when we don't make sound decisions, we allow our emotions to get the best of us within our life because we want to prove that we are adults that we can do things for ourselves. There are times when we need outside sources to lead us in the right direction or someone to confide with that can uplift us and change our minds to do the right thing. Instead, we choose to reason with ourselves and find our own way or path to how we conclude.

One of the questions I will ask myself is am I making a rational decision that will not cost me to lose out of what I am pursuing. Not making the right decision can lead a person to a sunken place of anxiety or depression. Overthinking will lead to thinking illogically. If an individual was in a relationship, they would have to understand that a good relationship coach or counselor can help them find a middle ground or arrive at a certain conclusion.

In order to come to making a good decision a person would want to meet a certain particular goal.

Steps to making good decisions:

- Ask for a second opinion.
- Gather information or other resources.
- If something was to happen, what would go wrong?
- What are the pros and cons?

This is why you must have a listening ear whenever you are in a conversation with someone that you want to help. Decision making is a two-way street especially for those who are in long-term relationships. It's about getting to the point of understanding one another's perspective of things. When a couple doesn't understand each other's point of view frustration and resentment begins to happen because they didn't carefully clarify to one another about the goals that they wanted with one another.

This is why having someone in your life that you can confide in is very important. The goal of having someone there to be with you is to listen to you sympathetically with care and concern.

LISTENING AS A FRIEND

You are to acknowledge what support they are seeking you for. Your position is to reflectively listen to what they have to say. Being able to understand their needs or concerns without interruption. Know when it is our turn to talk and not dominate the conversation. The problem with those who do not have a listening ear is that they do not show signs of respect for the person they are listening to that's telling their story. For them they just want to be heard. This is why coaching requires an individual to have good listening skills and individual must learn to listen attentively by responding and reflecting on what is being said by the person that they are confiding with. To listen to an individual who wants to be heard requires them to go deeper and what is being told. You have to find out what they are truly saying, what are the feelings that are being conveyed to you. It's all about absorbing that is coming in from the other person. Allow the person to feel comfortable when they are having a conversation with you to be open and honest without prejudice or judgment.

I know that when I am seeking a coach or a professional counselor, I'm looking for someone that I can trust because ultimately, I do understand that I want to be heard I will be looking for a coach that understands my own boundaries and show compassion towards me. It becomes a moment where I begin to express why I feel a certain way. There are so many people like me who just want someone to be there for them in the time of need. Mental health coaches become our support for the personal goals that we want to make in our lives. We want to be free from interference about everything else and just focus on the main issues dad we want to discuss.

The tips for mental health coaches to become a good listener.

- Were my feelings expressed?
- What were the person's concerns or thoughts about the conversation you had?
- Was the person that I had the conversation with trustworthy?
- Did you ask for clarification during the conversation on the subject matter?

THE ART OF BALANCING EMPATHY AND GUIDANCE:
NURTURING RELATIONSHIPS WITH A LISTENING EAR

When it comes to peoples connecting, there this great art – the art of balancing empathy and guidance. As we navigate the intricacies of relationships with our spouses, family, and friends, we find ourselves seeking to be both a listening ear and a guiding voice in the times of despair.

This journey is an essential aspect of nurturing these bonds, fostering understanding, and fostering growth. As we embark on an exploration of how the simple act of lending a compassionate ear to our loved ones can strengthen the fabric of our relationships, while also acknowledging the significance of offering gentle guidance when called upon.

What Does a Listening Ear Including Giving Guidance Implies?

 A listening ear implies more than just passively hearing words; it involves actively engaging with the speaker's emotions, thoughts, and concerns. When we lend a listening ear to our spouse, family, and friends, we offer them a safe space to express themselves without judgment.

On the other hand, giving guidance entails providing thoughtful and constructive advice when the situation calls for it. As a guide, we offer insights and perspectives that can help our loved ones navigate challenges or make informed decisions. However, it's crucial to strike a delicate balance, ensuring that our guidance is offered with empathy and respect for their autonomy.

How To Give A Listening Ear To Our Spouses, Family, And Friends

1. Be fully present: When engaging in conversations with our loved ones, put aside distractions and focus solely on the interaction. Show genuine interest and maintain eye contact to convey that you are attentive and invested in what they have to say.
2. Practice active listening: Listen not just to the words spoken but also to the emotions and underlying messages. Reflect on what they share and validate their feelings by acknowledging their experiences.
3. Avoid interrupting: Allow them to express themselves fully before offering any input. Interrupting can make them feel unheard and may hinder the flow of meaningful communication.
4. Be non-judgmental: Create a safe space where they feel comfortable expressing their thoughts and concerns without fear of judgment.
5. Avoid rushing to solve problems: Sometimes, people simply need to vent or express their emotions without seeking immediate solutions. Offer support and reassurance before providing guidance or advice.
6. Be patient and supportive: Understand that people may take time to open up or share their feelings. Be patient and supportive, letting them know you are there for them whenever they are ready.

How To Give Guidance To Others Who Are Not Your Relatives

1. Build trust: Establish a foundation of trust and rapport with the person before offering guidance. Show genuine interest in their well-being and demonstrate that you have their best interests at heart.
2. Listen actively: Before giving guidance, listen carefully to their concerns and needs. Understand their perspective and the challenges they are facing.
3. Offer empathy and understanding: Show compassion and empathy towards their situation, acknowledging their emotions and validating their experiences.
4. Be respectful and non-judgmental: Avoid being critical or judgmental about their choices or actions. Create a supportive environment where they feel comfortable opening up.
5. Share your experiences: If relevant, share your own experiences and how you navigated similar challenges. This can provide them with valuable insights and reassurance that they are not alone.
6. Provide objective feedback: Offer honest and constructive feedback, focusing on the issue at hand rather than personal attacks. Be specific and clear in your advice.

7. Encourage self-reflection: Help them explore their thoughts and feelings about the situation, guiding them to find their solutions and empowering them in the decision-making process.

8. Follow-up and support: After providing guidance, follow up with them to see how they are doing. Offer ongoing support and encouragement as they work through their challenges.

AVOID OVERFAMILIARITY

Maintaining a healthy boundary and avoiding familiarity when offering guidance to someone who is not your relative is crucial to ensure a professional and respectful relationship. Here are some ways to achieve that:

1. **Stay objective:** Focus on the specific issue or challenge at hand rather than getting too emotionally involved. Keep the conversation centered on their needs and concerns.
2. **Respect their privacy:** Avoid prying into their personal life or asking intrusive questions. Let them share what they feel comfortable sharing, and refrain from delving into sensitive topics unrelated to the guidance.
3. **Maintain a professional demeanor:** Approach the interaction with a level of professionalism and maturity. Be mindful of your tone and language, ensuring it remains appropriate and respectful.
4. **Set clear boundaries:** Define the scope of your guidance and let them know the limits of your involvement. Make it clear that while you are there to support them, you are not responsible for their decisions or actions.
5. **Limit personal sharing:** While sharing your experiences can be helpful, avoid oversharing or making the conversation primarily about yourself. The focus should be on their needs and growth.
6. **Avoid favoritism:** Treat everyone you offer guidance to with fairness and equal consideration. Avoid forming close personal attachments that may compromise your objectivity.

7. **Practice active listening:** Listen attentively to their concerns without making assumptions or jumping to conclusions. Be patient and let them express themselves fully.

8. **Be mindful of body language:** Non-verbal cues can inadvertently convey familiarity. Maintain a respectful distance and avoid overly casual gestures or physical contact.

9. **Know when to refer them elsewhere:** If their situation requires expertise beyond your capacity, be willing to recommend professional help or refer them to appropriate resources.

HOW TO BALANCE THE TWO CONCEPTS

Balancing the concepts of being a listening ear and offering guidance requires finesse and sensitivity to ensure one complements the other without causing conflicts. Here's how to achieve this harmonious balance:

1. **Timing is key:** Know when to listen empathetically and when to offer guidance. Sometimes, people just need someone to listen to and validate their feelings without seeking immediate solutions. Other times, they may be open to receiving advice or suggestions.

2. **Ask for permission:** Before giving guidance, ask if they are open to hearing your thoughts or suggestions. Respecting their willingness to receive guidance ensures you don't impose unsolicited advice.

3. **Be non-directive:** Instead of telling them what to do, guide them through reflective questions that prompt self-discovery and decision-making. Encourage them to explore their feelings and thoughts, empowering them to find solutions on their own.

4. **Separate roles:** Clearly distinguish between being a listening ear and providing guidance. Ensure they understand the difference in these roles and that you intend to support them in the best way possible.

5. **Avoid overstepping boundaries:** Respect their autonomy and refrain from taking control of their decisions. The guidance you provide should be supportive and not dictatorial.

6. **Stay empathetic:** Even when offering guidance, maintain empathy and understanding. Show that you genuinely care about their well-being and that your advice comes from a place of compassion.

7. **Be open to their perspective:** While offering guidance, be open to learning from their experiences and perspectives. Be willing to adapt your approach, if necessary, based on their unique circumstances.
8. **Acknowledge their choices:** Once they make decisions based on your guidance or their reflections, respect their choices, whether they align with your suggestions or not.

CONCLUSION

In conclusion, mastering the art of balancing empathy as a listening ear and offering guidance is a powerful skill in nurturing meaningful relationships. By actively listening with compassion and providing thoughtful guidance when needed, we can create a harmonious and supportive environment, enriching both our connections and personal growth.

Scriptural References

1. Proverbs 18:13 - "To answer before listening—that is folly and shame." This verse highlights the importance of actively listening and understanding before offering guidance.

2. James 1:19 - "My dear brothers and sisters, take note of this: Everyone should be quick to listen, slow to speak, and slow to become angry." This verse emphasizes the significance of patient and empathetic listening in our interactions with others.

3. Proverbs 15:22 - "Plans fail for lack of counsel, but with many advisers, they succeed." Seeking guidance from others and providing it in a supportive manner can lead to wiser decisions and successful outcomes.

4. Ephesians 4:29 - "Do not let any unwholesome talk come out of your mouths, but only what helps build others up according to their needs, that it may benefit those who listen." This verse reminds us to use our words to uplift and support others.

5. Galatians 6:2 - "Carry each other's burdens, and in this way, you will fulfill the law of Christ." Being a listening ear and offering guidance can be an expression of compassion and fulfilling the teachings of Christ.

LISTENING TO CHILDREN AS A MINISTER

As a minister the role is to support them. Recognizing the importance of listening to children is a step in the right direction. Here are some keys listening to children:

1. Before you become be a listening ear to someone where if they are an adult or young person you would want to ensure them that you will be trusted.
2. Listening to children empowers them and begin to have confidence when they are expressing themselves, they begin to feel respected and develop confidence within themselves.
3. They begin to build trust and feel a sense of comfort in an environment where the person that they are speaking with is trusted.
4. Children begin to have a sense of belonging when they feel that they are not being heard. You begin to understand their unique experiences about their current and past life way of living.
5. Listening to their concerns can help you develop unique ways of speaking to them that may impact them greatly in a positive way.
6. Listening to children can be very meaningful as you encourage the youth with a sense of understanding, collaboration with one another.
7. The most important thing that you can do is value their perspectives about what they have to tell you without judging them.

Why Is Listening Important In Pastoral Counseling?

Listening is a major part of pastoral counseling, it's the cornerstone when it comes to building trust and spiritual growth. Pastoral counselors, often situated within religious or spiritual contexts, support individuals that grapple with a wide range of emotional and spiritual concerns. Listening plays an important role in creating a safe environment where individuals can share their thoughts, feelings, and spiritual beliefs.

One of the primary reasons why listening is so helpful in pastoral counseling is its ability to cultivate a deep sense of understanding and empathy. Pastoral counselors strive to meet individuals where they are. By listening nonjudgmentally, counselors demonstrate genuine care and concern for their clients, laying the foundation for meaningful exploration and growth.

Pastoral counseling goes beyond mere acknowledgment of verbal communication. Many individuals seek pastoral counseling specifically for support to seek purpose in their lives. Effective listening allows counselors to understand individuals that have spiritual struggles within their life and gives them guidance and support based on their needs.

Pastoral counselors do not impose their own beliefs on those who seek spiritual guidance from them but rather they allow the client to open up to them about their purpose beliefs and faith.

When it comes to active listening counselors and power parishioners or clients that wrestle with questions that they won't answer concerning their spiritual walk so that they can move forward in life. The pastoral counselor and client is a collaborative approach between one another.

Listening also serves as a vehicle for healing and transformation in pastoral counseling. As clients share their stories, struggles, and spiritual aspirations, they often experience a sense of relief and validation. Furthermore, listening in pastoral counseling facilitates discernment and guidance in navigating ethical dilemmas, moral conflicts, and difficult life decisions.

In summary, listening is invaluable in pastoral counseling for its capacity to foster understanding, empathy, empowerment, healing, and spiritual growth. Through attentive presence, empathetic attunement, and respectful engagement, pastoral counselors create a sacred space where individuals can explore their innermost thoughts, emotions, and spiritual aspirations. By honoring the client's autonomy, facilitating meaningful dialogue, and offering guidance rooted in spiritual wisdom, counselors support individuals on their journey towards wholeness, authenticity, and spiritual flourishing.

How Has Not Listening Effect People In Society

Having a listening ear is crucial in society because it fosters empathy, understanding, and support. Without it, individuals may feel isolated, misunderstood, and unsupported, leading to issues like loneliness, mental health struggles, and strained relationships. Additionally, the absence of a listening ear can hinder effective communication and problem-solving, making it harder for communities to address shared challenges and work together towards common goals.

Overcoming the habit of not listening requires conscious effort and practice. Here are some tips:

1. **Be present:** at least be actively engaged with the person that you are having conversations with.
2. **Practice active listening:** Listen attentively, ask clarifying questions, and provide feedback to show that you understand.
3. **Empathize:** Put yourself in the speaker's shoes to understand their perspective and feelings.
4. **Be open-minded:** Avoid jumping to conclusions or forming judgments prematurely.

5. **Manage distractions:** Minimize interruptions and distractions, such as turning off electronic devices or finding a quiet environment.
6. **Reflect on your listening habits:** observe your own listening skills so that you may improve in the areas that you may feel weak at.
7. **Seek feedback:** try to ask them for feedback based on what they understand and use constructive criticism.
8. **Practice patience:** always allow them to express themselves and for them to speak when they can
9. **Be genuine:** try to support them by showing them genuine concern
10. **Practice mindfulness:** practice mindfulness and allow them to be aware that you are listening to them

By incorporating these strategies into your daily interactions, you can gradually improve your listening skills and become a more attentive and empathetic communicator.

LISTENING AS A MINISTER VERSUS A COACH

Listening is a fundamental aspect of effective communication, regardless of the context. However, the role of listening differs significantly between being a minister and being a life coach. While both professions involve providing support and guidance to individuals, the objectives, methods, and outcomes of listening vary based on the unique responsibilities and goals of each role.

As a minister, listening is primarily focused on spiritual and emotional support. Ministers often listen to congregants during counseling sessions, sermons, or pastoral care visits. In this context, listening is deeply rooted in empathy, compassion, and understanding. A minister listens not only to the words spoken but also to the emotions, beliefs, and values underlying those words. They provide a safe space for individuals to express their thoughts, concerns, and struggles, without fear of judgment or condemnation.

Moreover, listening as a minister involves interpreting and reflecting on the religious or spiritual aspects of the conversation. Ministers may draw upon their knowledge of scripture, theology, and religious teachings to offer guidance, comfort, and encouragement. They listen not only with their ears but also with their hearts, seeking to discern the divine presence and guidance in the lives of those they serve.

On the other hand, listening as a life coach is more focused on personal development and goal achievement. Life coaches listen to clients in one-on-one sessions, workshops, or seminars, with the aim of helping them clarify their goals, overcome obstacles, and achieve greater fulfillment in their lives. Listening in this context is goal-oriented and action-oriented, with an emphasis on active listening techniques such as paraphrasing, reflecting, and clarifying.

Life coaches listen to their clients' desires, aspirations, and challenges, helping them explore their values, beliefs, and priorities. Through attentive listening, life coaches help clients gain insights into their strengths, weaknesses, and areas for growth. They ask powerful questions that prompt clients to reflect deeply, challenge limiting beliefs, and develop strategies for success.

Furthermore, listening as a life coach often involves holding clients accountable for their actions and commitments. Coaches help clients set specific, measurable, achievable, relevant, and time-bound (SMART) goals and support them in taking consistent action towards their goals. Listening in this context is not passive but dynamic and transformative, empowering clients to take ownership of their lives and create meaningful change.

In summary, while both ministers and life coaches engage in listening as part of their professional practice, the nature and objectives of listening differ significantly between the two roles. As a minister, listening is rooted in empathy, compassion, and spiritual discernment, with a focus on providing spiritual and emotional support to individuals. In contrast, listening as a life coach is goal-oriented and action-oriented, aimed at helping clients clarify their goals, overcome obstacles, and achieve greater fulfillment in their lives. Despite these differences, both professions recognize the transformative power of listening in fostering growth, healing, and empowerment in the lives of those they serve.

Cultivating Active Listening For Stronger Relationships

As humans we make connections with one another through human interaction we learned that listening helps us to become more understanding and pathetic with people involved in our lives. The art of listening often gets overshadowed by many distractions. To enrich our relationships, we must become better in the skill of active listening. Listening will help you build practical strategies to become a better listener in relationships, make meaningful connections and growth.

The foundation of effective listening in a world where technology seems to be the norm for communication in a conversation can be a rarity. To become a better listener, one must cultivate mindfulness anchoring attention to the here and now we must learn to set aside distractions and give our undivided attention to them. We must engage with them by becoming attuned with them knowing about verbal cues and nonverbal expressions. Listening sometimes involves validation and empathy will you learn about a person's experiences and their emotions. You begin to learn about their sense of self-worth so that we can learn to trust them, and they can learn to trust you. You are not in the place to agree with everything that they must say to you but for you to gain a sense of sentiment by acknowledging their perspective and take everything that they would say to you for consideration.

As a listener I would want you to try to block out any area that may bring any judgment when you are engaging in a conversation with them because we may formulate any perceptions about what they tell us so we must set aside biases and become open with curiosity without any impulse to judge them so we must learn to create a safe space for them to express themselves. This is also a teaching moment that brings vulnerability and growth for you and for them without the absence of judgment. When there is an absence of judgment the person may feel empowered to share all that they want to express to you.

You will be faced with individuals who may bring insecurity issues or have emotional baggage. This would be your opportunity to help them self-reflect on where they are and where they want to be.

Furthermore, for you to become an excellent listener you must learn to be patient and have tolerance. You have to have patience to show some sort of receptivity and not to dismiss them where they may show different perspectives and opinions you will also not impede their understanding of a particular subject. The dialog must be respectful and embrace them with love and care.

How To Listen To Your Spouse When They Aren't Listening To You

When your spouse isn't listening, it can be incredibly frustrating and challenging to manage. However, effective communication is crucial for fostering understanding and resolving conflicts. Here are some strategies to help you listen to your partner when they aren't listening to you:

Stay Calm

It's natural to feel frustrated or upset when you feel unheard, but responding with anger and defensiveness can escalate the situation. Take a deep breath and try to stay calm before addressing the issue.

Choose Your Time Wisely

Timing is a crucial factor in dealing with communication issues. Choose a time when you and your partner are both calm and free of distractions. Avoid bringing up the problem in the middle of an argument or when your partner is preoccupied or stressed.

USE "I FEEL" STATEMENTS

Rather than pointing fingers or placing blame, express your feelings using "I feel" statements. For example, say, "I feel frustrated when I don't feel heard," instead of, "You never listen to me." This approach helps convey your emotions without making your partner feel attacked.

BE CLEAR AND SPECIFIC

When discussing the behavior or situation that is bothering you, be clear and specific. Use concrete examples to help your partner understand your point. This clarity can help them see the issue from your perspective.

PRACTICE ACTIVE LISTENING

Even if your partner isn't listening to you, practice active listening and validate their feelings. Acknowledge their emotions and perspective to help diffuse tension and create a more receptive atmosphere for communication.

SET BOUNDARIES

If your partner consistently ignores or dismisses your concerns, it may be necessary to set boundaries around communication. Let them know that you are open and willing to discuss issues, but ignoring each other's concerns is not acceptable. Setting these boundaries can help establish a healthier communication dynamic.

By staying calm, choosing the right time to talk, using "I feel" statements, being clear and specific, practicing active listening, and setting boundaries, you can improve your communication and foster a more understanding and supportive relationship.

Listening To Your Spouse's Heart Without Her Speaking

What I have come to learn is that in any relationship, especially marriage is that communication can often be heralded as the cornerstone of a healthy and enduring partnership. Verbal communication is an equally important aspect that often goes unspoken: in a marriage or if you are in a relationship, you will have the ability to listen to your spouse's heart without words. This skill involves being attuned to non-verbal cues, understanding their emotions by responding with empathy and support. Developing this skill can lead to deeper intimacy and trust. Let's explore how to listen to your spouse's heart without her speaking, covering the importance of non-verbal communication that could enhance our understanding, and the benefits this brings to a relationship.

Learning to use nonverbal communication can be a powerful tool for your understanding when it comes to connecting with your spouse. Especially when it comes to body language and facial expressions. You will have to come to a point where you will gain insight without the need for words about him or her.

As you get to know her or him you will have moments where you will be able to observe her facial expressions and body posture These are cues Insight That you will learn About The emotional State You will have to learn about the range of different emotions that they possess Such as discomfort Happiness Frustration or sadness Period

Even in the absence of words, the tone and pitch of sounds she makes— whether it's a hum, a sigh, or changes in her breathing patterns—can convey significant emotional information. A sigh, for instance, might indicate relief, frustration, or sadness, depending on the context. By being attentive to these auditory signals, you can better gauge how she is feeling.

One of the most important aspects of listening to your spouse's heart is being fully present. This means giving her your undivided attention when she is around. Put away distractions like phones, turn off the TV, and make eye contact. Being present shows that you value her and are genuinely interested in her well-being. It also creates an environment where she feels safe and understood, which can encourage her to open up non-verbally.

Context is crucial in interpreting non-verbal cues accurately. Understanding what is happening in your spouse's life can provide context for her emotions and behaviors. For instance, if she has had a particularly stressful day at work, her silence might be a need for quiet rather than an indication of anger. By being aware of the external factors affecting her, you can better understand her non-verbal signals and respond appropriately.

Try to understand that empathy is the ability to understand and share the feelings of another person. When you empathize with your spouse, you are putting yourself in her shoes and trying to feel what she is feeling. You begin to learn that there is an emotional connection to as a fundamental part of listening to her heart. To practice empathy you must pay close attention to her emotional cues and imagine how you would feel in her situation. Empathetic listening goes beyond just hearing words; it involves feeling and understanding emotional state.

How about physical touch which is basically a powerful form of non-verbal communication. A gentle touch of just holding hands can convey love and support. When words are insufficient or unnecessary, physical touch can bridge the gap. It reassures your spouse that you are there for her and that you care deeply. Be mindful of her preferences and comfort levels with touch and use it to communicate your support and affection.

Any relationship actions speak louder than words. Performing small acts of service that you know she appreciates can show that you understand and care for her needs. This could be making her favorite meal, taking care of household chores, or planning a relaxing evening together. These gestures demonstrate your commitment and attentiveness to her well-being, reinforcing your connection without the need for verbal communication.

Developing the ability to listen to your spouse's heart without her speaking brings numerous benefits to a relationship because it fosters intimacy and connection. When you understand and respond to your spouse's non-verbal cues, she feels valued and understood. At this point you begin to build trust. When your spouse knows that you can understand her without words, she feels more secure in the relationship. By being attuned to her feelings, you can provide the right kind of support when she needs the most.

Listening to your spouse's heart without her speaking is an essential skill that can enhance your relationship. It requires attentiveness and a genuine desire to understand her non-verbally. By observing body language, paying attention to tone and pitch, being present, understanding context, practicing empathy, using physical touch, and performing acts of service, you can connect with your spouse on a deeper emotional level. This non-verbal communication fosters intimacy, builds trust, and provides emotional support, creating a strong and enduring bond. Ultimately, by listening to your spouse's heart, you nurture a relationship built on understanding, respect, and love.

HEALING FROM LISTENING TO THE PEOPLE WHO WRONGED YOU

Healing from listening to the people who wronged you can be hard for so many of us. This process often requires courage, and the willingness to confront truths. It is a path that not only aims to mend the wounds inflicted by others but also seeks personal growth and deeper understanding of yourself. Your healing process may take time and involve several key elements: empathy, forgiveness, communication, and self-reflection.

To begin with, empathy plays a crucial role in this healing journey. Empathy is the ability to understand and share the feelings of another. When we listen to those who have wronged us, we are challenged to step into their shoes and see the world from their perspective. This doesn't mean justifying their actions or absolving them of responsibility, but rather trying to understand the motivations and circumstances that led to their behavior. For example, someone who was hurtful might have been acting out of their own pain or insecurity. By recognizing this, we can begin to humanize them, which can soften the edges of our own hurt and open the door to healing. This empathic approach can transform our perception of the situation, shifting from a binary of victim and perpetrator to a more nuanced understanding of two flawed humans navigating complex emotions and circumstances.

Forgiveness is another healing process, and it often goes hand-in-hand with empathy. True forgiveness is not about condoning the wrong or forgetting it ever happened. Instead, it is about releasing what's inside of us that may hold the past has on us, freeing ourselves from the grip of resentment. When we listen to those who have wronged us, we may hear apologies or explanations that help us understand their actions better. This understanding can pave the way to forgiveness, as it allows us to see the person behind the action. Forgiveness is ultimately a gift we give ourselves, as it unburdens our heart and mind from the toxic weight of grudges and bitterness.

Effective communication is integral to this healing process. Engaging in open and honest dialogue with the person who wronged us can be incredibly cathartic. It provides a platform for expressing our hurt and pain, and for the other person to offer their perspective and possibly an apology. Such conversations, however, require a safe and respectful environment. It is important to set boundaries and ensure that the discussion remains constructive. Active listening, where both parties genuinely try to understand each other without interrupting or becoming defensive, is essential. This form of communication can help both parties to process their emotions and to start rebuilding trust, even if it's just a small step.

Self-reflection is another vital component of healing from such interactions. It involves introspection and a deep examination of our own responses, feelings, and behaviors. Through self-reflection, we can identify our triggers, understand why certain actions hurt us so deeply, and recognize patterns in our emotional responses. This awareness can empower us to handle future conflicts better. It can help us to see our own role in the dynamic. While it is crucial not to blame ourselves for being wronged, understanding how we might have contributed to the situation can be enlightening and can help us to grow emotionally.

The journey of healing through listening to those who have wronged can be challenging. It involves confronting the pain of your past head-on, which can be daunting. Yet, this process can lead to personal growth and liberation from your past. By opening ourselves up to understanding and potentially forgiving those who hurt us, we are not only seeking closure but also reclaiming our own power and agency. We are reclaiming what the enemy has stolen from us. We are choosing to let go of the past That once had a mighty grip on our lives in the past but now we have allowed the Holy Spirit to take over our lives by allowing us to move forward.

Moreover, this healing journey can transform relationships. In some cases, it can lead to reconciliation and a stronger bond. In other instances, it might mean redefining the relationship or even letting it go but doing so from a place of peace rather than resentment. Once you have become healed from any past situations it will help your emotional well-being and your overall outlook on life, especially your past relationships.

Healing from listening to the people who wronged us is a process that involves forgiveness, and self-reflection. It is a path that requires courage and personal growth and freedom. By understanding and forgiving those who hurt us, we not only heal our wounds, but we also pave the way for a better you.

This helped me in my personal life to forgive those who I know who have wronged me on a personal level and I have done so much and have come so far on this journey. If it wasn't for God I wouldn't know where I would be today and I thank God for all that he has done in my life.

50 Tools To Become A Better Listener

1. **Active Listening:** Try to focus completely on the speaker, acknowledging their words with nods and verbal affirmations.
2. Use Eye Contact: Maintain appropriate eye contact to show interest and engagement.
3. **Paraphrasing What You Are Going To Say:** Restate what the speaker has said in your own words to confirm understanding. 4.
4. Summarizing: Briefly recap the main points of the conversation to ensure clarity.
5. **Ask Open-Ended Questions:** Ask questions that require more than a yes/no answer to encourage detailed responses.
6. **Clarification:** Request clarification on points that are unclear to ensure accurate understanding.
7. **Empathy:** Show empathy by expressing understanding and sharing similar experiences.
8. **Non-Verbal Cues:** Use facial expressions and gestures to show attentiveness and understanding.
9. **Avoid Interrupting:** Let the speaker finish their thoughts before responding.
10. **Reflective Listening:** Reflect on what is being said by repeating back the speaker's message.

11. **Active Feedback:** Provide feedback that shows you are engaged and understand the conversation.
12. **Notetaking:** Jot down key points during important conversations to remember details.
13. **Patience:** Allow the speaker to express their thoughts fully without rushing them.
14. **Tone of Voice:** Use a calm and respectful tone to foster a positive listening environment.
15. **Mindfulness:** Stay present in the moment and focus on the conversation without letting your mind wander.
16. **Body Language:** Use open body language to show you are receptive and attentive.
17. **Validation:** Validate the speaker's feelings and experiences to show that you understand and respect their perspective.
18. Non-Judgmental Attitude: Listen without forming judgments or opinions prematurely.
19. **Minimal Encouragers:** Use small verbal prompts like "I see," "Go on," or "Really?" to encourage the speaker to continue.
20. Avoid Distractions: Eliminate potential distractions like phones or other electronic devices during conversations.
21. **Cultural Sensitivity:** Be aware of and respect cultural differences in communication styles.
22. **Listening for Emotions:** Pay attention to the emotional undertones in the speaker's words.
23. **Positive Reinforcement:** Encourage the speaker by acknowledging their effort and insights.
24. **Summarize Agreements:** Summarize points of agreement to build mutual understanding.
25. **Focus on Intent:** Try to understand the speaker's intentions and motivations behind their words.
26. **Avoid Personal Biases:** Be aware of your own biases and try to listen objectively.
27. **Open Body Posture:** Use an open and relaxed posture to show that you are approachable and engaged.

28. **Stay Calm:** Maintain a calm demeanor, even if the conversation becomes tense or emotional.
29. **Restate Key Points:** Periodically restate key points to ensure mutual understanding.
30. **Acknowledge Non-Verbal Signals:** Recognize and respond to the speaker's non-verbal cues.
31. **Time Management:** Allocate sufficient time for important conversations without feeling rushed.
32. **Practice Empathy Statements:** Use statements like "I understand how you feel" to show empathy.
33. **Avoid Multitasking:** You don't want to be focusing solely on the conversation without trying to do other tasks simultaneously.
34. **Encourage Sharing:** Try to create a safe space for the speaker to share openly and honestly.
35. **Be Open-Minded:** You must be open to new ideas and perspectives without immediately dismissing them.
36. **Ask for Examples:** Request specific examples to better understand abstract or complex points.
37. **Control Emotional Reactions:** Keep your emotions in check to listen more effectively.
38. **Provide Constructive Feedback:** Offer feedback that is supportive and helps the speaker improve.
39. **Respect Silence:** Allow for pauses and moments of silence as the speaker collects their thoughts.
40. **Show Genuine Interest:** Demonstrate genuine interest in the speaker's message through your words and actions.
41. **Avoid Assumptions:** Don't assume you know what the speaker is going to say; let them express themselves fully.
42. **Be Receptive to Criticism:** Listen openly to constructive criticism without becoming defensive.
43. **Reframe From Negative Comments:** Reframe negative statements in a more positive or neutral light.
44. **Acknowledge Their Perspectives:** Recognize and validate differing viewpoints.

45. **Summarize What You Have to Say Before Responding:** Summarize the speaker's points before offering your own input.
46. **Practice Patience:** Give the speaker time to articulate their thoughts without interrupting.
47. **Stay Objective At All Times:** Focus on the content of the conversation rather than personal feelings.
48. **Try To Not Dominate the Conversation:** Ensure the speaker has ample opportunity to share their thoughts.
49. **Follow Up:** Follow up on important points or commitments made during the conversation.
50. **Continuous Improvement:** Regularly seek feedback on your listening skills and strive to improve them.

MENTAL HEALTH RESOURCES FOR COUNSELING ASSISTANCE

Here are ten mental health resources for counseling assistance and ten resources for general mental health help:

COUNSELING ASSISTANCE:

1. **BetterHelp:** Offers online counseling with licensed therapists.
2. **Talkspace:** Provides online therapy with licensed therapists via text, audio, and video messaging.
3. **7 Cups:** Offers free online therapy and counseling through trained listeners and licensed therapists.
4. **Psychology Today:** Has a directory of therapists, psychiatrists, and support groups searchable by location and specialty.
5. **National Alliance on Mental Illness (NAMI):** Provides support groups and resources for individuals and families affected by mental illness.
6. **Therapist Locator by the American Psychological Association:** Helps you find licensed psychologists in your area.
7. **Open Path Collective:** Offers affordable in-person and online therapy sessions with licensed therapists.
8. **Institute of Mental Health (IMH):** Provides a wide range of mental health services including counseling and therapy.

9. **SAMHSA National Helpline:** Offers 24/7 free and confidential treatment referral and information service for mental health and substance use disorders.

10. **Online-Therapy.com:** Provides online cognitive behavioral therapy (CBT) programs with licensed therapists.

GENERAL MENTAL HEALTH HELP:

1. **National Suicide Prevention Lifeline:** Provides free and confidential emotional support to people in suicidal crisis or emotional distress.

2. **2.Crisis Text Line:** Offers free, 24/7 support for those in crisis via text messaging.

3. **MentalHealth.gov:** Offers resources, information, and guidance on various mental health topics.

4. **Anxiety and Depression Association of America (ADAA):** Provides resources, support groups, and information on anxiety and depression.

5. **5.Substance Abuse and Mental Health Services Administration (SAMHSA):** Offers resources and support for mental health and substance abuse disorders.

6. **Mind:** Provides advice and support to empower anyone experiencing a mental health problem.

7. **National Institute of Mental Health (NIMH):** Offers information on mental health disorders, research, and clinical trials.

8. **Mental Health America (MHA):** Provides resources, screenings, and advocacy for mental health awareness.

9. **Headspace:** Offers guided meditation and mindfulness exercises to help with stress, anxiety, and other mental health concerns.

10. **Rethink Mental Illness:** Offers support and information for people affected by mental illness and their families.